BULLY!

The Big Book About Bullies and the Bullied

MUCH OF THE POETRY IN THIS BOOK FIRST APPEARED IN THE FOLLOWING:
Scents of Place (Country Messenger Press – Marine, Minnesota, 1987 – Out of Print)
In-Versing Your Life (Blooming Twig Books – New York, 2006 – ISBN 978-0-9777736-9-5)
Fe-Vers for Children (Blooming Twig Books – New York, 2006 – ISBN 978-1-933918-01-3)
Fe-Vers for Teens (Blooming Twig Books – New York, 2006 – ISBN 978-1-933918-02-0)
Re-Versing the Numbers (Blooming Twig Books – New York, 2006 – ISBN 978-0-9777736-8-8)
Re-Versing Your Pain (Blooming Twig Books – New York, 2006 – ISBN 978-0-9777736-7-1)
Con-Versing with God (Blooming Twig Books – New York, 2006 – ISBN 978-1-933918-00-6)
Please Use This for Children (Blooming Twig Books – New York, 2010 – ISBN 978-1-933918-50-1)

BULLY!
Copyright © 2011 Cynthia Gustavson
www.cynthiagustavson.com

Cover Illustration by Kristina Tosic
www.eskalicka.com

Interior Illustrations by Kent Gustavson
www.kentgustavson.com

Published by:
Blooming Twig Books
320 S. Boston Suite 1026 / Tulsa, OK 74103
Tel: 1-866-398-1482
www.bloomingtwig.com

Print Edition   ISBN 978-1-61343-001-9
Ebook Edition   ISBN 978-1-61343-005-7

Printed in the United States of America

BULLY!

The Big Book About Bullies and the Bullied

Cynthia Blomquist Gustavson, ACSW, LCSW

with **Kent Gustavson**, PhD

Foreword by **Dr. Edward E. Gustavson**, MD, FAAP

BLOOMING TWIG BOOKS

NEW YORK / TULSA

TABLE OF CONTENTS

FOREWORD

In my pediatric practice, I am frequently sent children who cannot or will not talk, who are defined as "loners" or "losers", who are seen repeatedly by the school nurse, are often sent home from school, and have high absence rates. Many of these children have problems with their schoolmates, especially at lunch, on the playground, and in their mandatory physical education classes. I have found that the majority of children hate certain games that are common in nearly every phy-ed program; especially dodgeball and football. Within these two particular sports, bullies prevail, and they are unfortunately also often supervised by adult bullies.

Bullying is increasing within *every* community, and after working in three regions of the United States and seeing all ages of children, my experience is that bullying begins as early as preschool for some. Here are a few recent statistics:

- Nearly half of schoolchildren report being bullied.

- Boys engage in more physical and verbal bullying, and girls participate in more social bullying.

- About 10% of elementary-aged children report bullying within the previous two month period.

- Children with learning problems, physical disabilities, gender and social differences are more frequent victims.

For more than twenty years, studies of the outcomes of bullying on the victims report the following (when compared with non-bullied children):

- Bullied children have four times the incidence of depression.

- Bullied children have three times the normal rate of both abdominal pain and anxiety.

- Bullied children have almost seven times the incidence of bed wetting.

- In a study of children with psychiatric problems, bullied children had double the problems with serious mental illness, substance abuse and chronic institutional management.

The severity of bullying has increased in parallel to the breakdown of traditional communication; physicians, psychologists and researchers all agree that families are under social and financial pressures. I implore you to join me in the fight against bullying. Because children grow up within varied home surroundings, it is vital that children be shepherded and mentored by teachers and other responsible adult figures.

The rising tide of awareness around the issue of bullying brought forth by recent tragedies and by an anti-bullying agenda in the current White House has brought us a few more steps towards the goal of a safer environment for our children. However, there is a long way to go; teachers and administrators should team with parents, psychologists, physicians and anyone at the table in order to work towards real and lasting change.

Read this book and promote the wellbeing of our children; *especially* the vulnerable and most sensitive. They *will* be our future leaders.

Dr. Edward Gustavson, MD, FAAP
Developmental Pediatrician

INTRODUCTION

FOR PARENTS & TEACHERS

Bullying is a hot topic in America today, and with good reason. Every school, group of friends, and family has someone who has been a victim of bullying, and most have someone who has acted like a bully. We all know bullying only *starts* in childhood, and it carries along from there to workplaces, relationships, and everywhere else in our modern world.

As a practicing psychotherapist, I have treated both bully and victim, and have tried many different approaches in counseling both. It is *very* important not only to counsel the bullied, but also to work with the bullies themselves. I have designed this book to address both sides of the problem. Many of these writing exercises originated in my two previous workbooks, *Fe-Vers: Feeling Verses for Children,* and *Fe-Vers: Feeling Verses for Teens* (2006 Blooming Twig Books).

Bullying can be physical, it can be purely psychological, or a combination of the two. For purposes of this book I will discuss a little about the physical type of bullying, but will mainly concentrate on the psychological aspects of bullying. The definition of bullying I will use is: when someone takes advantage of unequal power for the bully's own ends, and the bullied individual is left in a worse state.

As teachers, parents and other responsible adults, we often don't know what to do except break up fights when we see them on the playground. What else can we do to protect the children in our care from physical bullying? Here are a few simple strategies to start with:

1. Teach the bullied child never to be alone when he/she would normally encounter a bully. The bullied are far less vulnerable when they are supported by friends and family. Much as a triangular structure such as an A-frame house has more strength, teaching the bullied to draw on a third person's strength will give them more power against the bully. If the bullied child knows that he/she will be attacked on the way to school, he or she should make sure that someone walks there with him/her every day.

2. Bullied children should call on authority figures to give themselves more power. Help bullied individuals feel safe in coming to you and other school officials, police, parents and others.

3. Carrying a cell phone is helpful. The victim can call for help, and (responsibly) transmit video or audio if they are being bullied.

4.   A fourth strategy that is difficult at first, but very effective over time is self-defense training. Not only does such physical training help the child actually defend themselves when attacked physically, but they also will reap the self-empowering benefits of the martial arts or other athletic practice that goes along with the training.

The most difficult role that I have had to play in instances of bullying is being a counselor to bullies. It is easy (and necessary) for us as parents and teachers to sympathize and reach out to the bullied children. But in our rush to assist the bullied, we often fail to counsel and coach the bullies. The methods contained within this book are proven to work with both bullies and bullied individuals, helping them to build inner strength as a defense against vulnerability to others. That inner strength, defined by characteristics such self-empowerment, understanding, patience, and compassion, will lead to assertiveness. Together, we will help build a new vision of the future.

INTRODUCTION

FOR THE KIDS

There was a little girl
who had a little curl
right in the middle of her forehead

And when she was good
she was very very good,
but when she was bad she was horrid.

– Henry Wadsworth Longfellow

D o you ever feel like the kid in this rhyme? Do you do what you're supposed to do most of the time, and act fine and proper, but every once in a while you get so angry or frustrated that you just can't be nice anymore? Or has someone ever treated you really badly, and you just exploded? Those explosions are where "bullying" comes from, no matter who we are.

Chances are we've all been a bully at some time or other, even if it was just being mean to our cat or stomping down the neighbor's flowers when they weren't watching. Have you ever done something like that?

Some of you will say, "Oh no, I've never been a bully," but chances are, you have been when you didn't even notice! Most of you have also been bullied by others, and have had to avoid certain people and places because of it.

What is a bully? What is it like to get bullied? It's not "bad" if you are either a bully or if you are bullied. Just about every one of us has been there! I've been bullied, and my son, who is now very tall, was once very small, and he was bullied all the time. But he grew up strong and assertive, and now he has a PhD, and he helped me to write this book!

Get ready to work. Get ready to see the world through different eyes. Get ready to change!

BULLIES

COME IN ALL SHAPES & SIZES!

On the following pages, there are eight cartoons of different kids. Do they look like bullies to you? Or do they look nice? Would they be your friends? Which ones? While you look at their pictures, think about what *you* look like to *other* people!

You will also see that there are places where you can draw a picture of yourself and someone else at the end of this section. It's okay if your drawing looks like a stick figure - it's almost more fun that way. Also, if you feel more comfortable drawing pictures instead of writing words anywhere in the book, please do that. We all express ourselves in different ways, and that's great!

FRANCES (FRANKIE)

Likes: cheerleading, swim team, boys, flute.

Picks on: overweight girls, geeks, her cat.

Bullied by: her dad when he drinks.

JAMES (HOSS)

Likes: football, pizza, parties, swimming.

Picks on: his younger brother, wimps.

Bullied by: his older brother & his friends.

JULIA (JULES-Y)

Likes: organic food, tattoos, hiking, dogs.

Picks on: cheerleaders, her boyfriend.

Bullied by: her physics teacher, her mom.

GEORGE (G.W.)

Likes: reading, playing tennis, studying.

Picks on: his little sister (sometimes).

Bullied by: jocks and jerks.

CHARLOTTE (CHAR)

Likes: volleyball, writing in her journal.

Picks on: her mom (sometimes).

Bullied by: the cool girls.

MARTIN (MARTY)

Likes: baseball, candy bars, school.

Picks on: ants and other small insects.

Bullied by: it seems like everyone.

EMILY (EMMY)

Likes: debate, cooking, swing dancing.

Picks on: her less intelligent friends.

Bullied by: skinny girls.

CHARLES (CHUCKY)

Likes: cars, basketball, weightlifting.

Picks on: geeks at school, his dog.

Bullied by: his mom and her boyfriends.

Fill in your own information below & sketch yourself above.

NAME:

Likes:

Picks on:

Bullied by:

Now, sketch someone who bullies you, or whom you pick on.

NAME:

Likes:

Picks on:

Bullied by:

Bully or Bullied?

In the poem *Under Nature's Wing* do you identify with the eagle, or the person who fell? Why?

Were you surprised that I stared back at the end of the poem, "daring" to look at the eagle?

Imagine you were in that situation, and write about what you would think and do.

IN THIS SITUATION I WOULD...

I'M NOT AFRAID OF THAT EAGLE!

Now think about *Under Nature's Wing* again, but pretend you are the eagle. What would your response be to the person on the ground? Are you a bully sometimes, like the eagle in this situation? Write about it below:

Which one are you *more* like? Eagle or skier? Write about it!

HOW DO YOU FEEL?

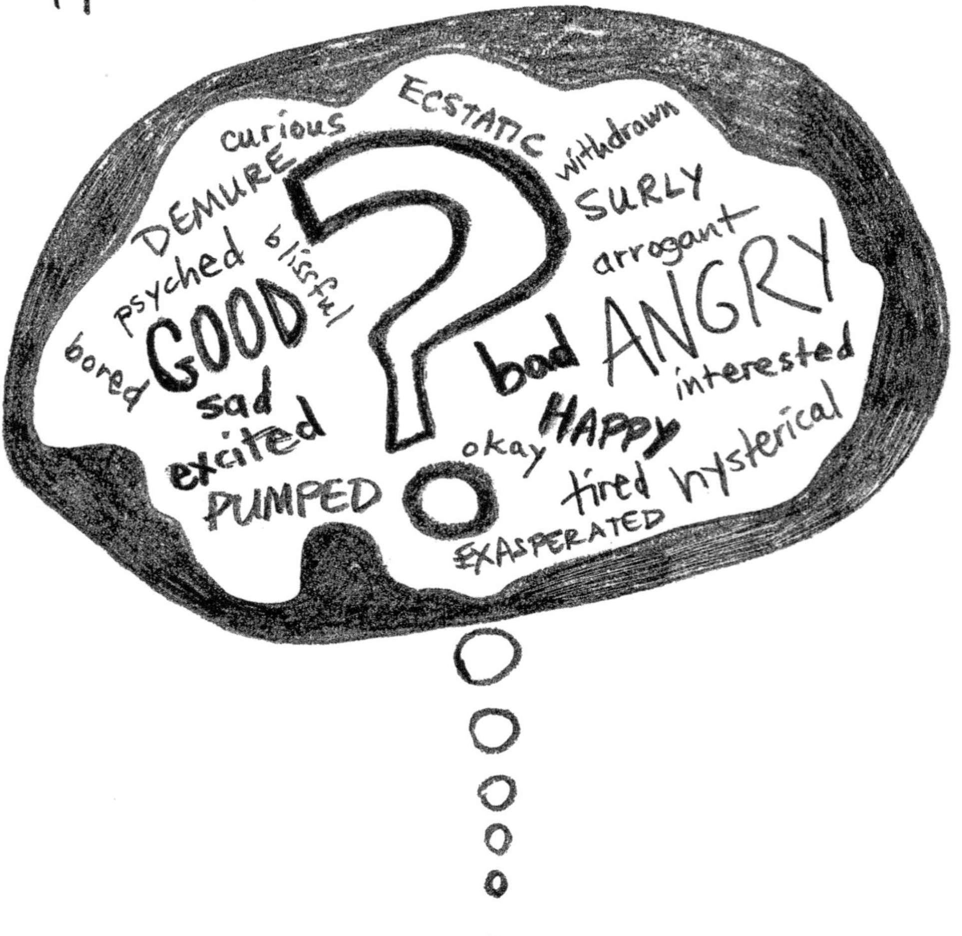

How do you feel?

When I was a kid if you had asked me how I felt, I would have answered with only a few words:

good,
bad,
sad,
happy.

I now understand there are countless words for all the different ways we might feel. The more words we use and get to know, the healthier we will become.

Think about all the different words in the poem on the next page that describe your feelings.

Look up the meanings of some of the words if you don't know them, or just want to have a clearer meaning!

Give yourself a reward if you are able to use these words throughout the day today!

How Do I Feel Today?

Is it exasperated, exhausted, pleased, enraged,
optimistic, pessimistic, detached or engaged?

Determined, disgusted, bashful or bored,
over-anxious, confident, blissful or ignored?

Apologetic, arrogant, agonized, smug,
pleased and peaceful as a bug on a rug?

Sometimes I feel as if I were demure,
but most of the time, I'm not really sure.

Today I am curious, idiotic, ecstatic,
envious, hysterical, and getting "combatic".

So don't you get cold or aggressive or surly,
or make me mad or wake me up early.

Tomorrow I might be meditative, withdrawn,
writing love letters while lying on the lawn.

Whatever I feel . . . it's okay with me.
(And by the way . . . You can disagree!)

Feelings OK... Actions *Not* Always OK

In *How Do I Feel Today* I say that it's okay to feel any way we want! I write "feel" and not "act" for a reason. Our feelings are very real, but that does not mean it is all right to act on those feelings all the time.

We choose our actions. That means something different to the bully and the bullied. The bully needs to curb his/her negative behavior towards others. The bullied needs to change his/her negative behavior towards him/herself.

If you are sometimes a bully, write down the words from the poem *How Do I Feel Today* that make you think your behavior might be okay. Now make a list below of non-hurtful things that you can do when you feel that way, and write more about it on the next page.

WORD LIST:

DO YOU GET PUSHED AROUND BY BULLIES?

Use the words in your two lists on the previous page and write about how you act, and whether or not that action is alright. How do you feel about it?

Now, write down all the words that you feel, and write them the **SIZE** that you feel them! Small, big, sideways - any way you like!

FEELING WORDS:

GREAT WORK!

IT'S NOT EASY BEING ~~GREEN~~ ME!

What mood are you in?

It is easy to express your emotions through poetry – that's why I have loved reading and writing since I was a small child in Minnesota.

I bet you can tell what kind of mood I was in when I wrote the *visual* poem on the following page! *All I Want* is one of my favorite kind of poems. They are very fun to write because they use not only words and the meaning and sounds of the words, but also how the words look on the page. As you can see in the poem, I am able to express a lot of emotions using just a few words on the page!

If you are interested in looking at other poems that are kind of like this one, you can check out a book of poetry by e.e. cummings, who was already writing this kind of poetry a long time before I was born! (Just ask a librarian, and they will help you find a book full of this great poetry.)

All I Want

all i want to do is

(hide)

all i want to do is

rrrrrrrrrrruuuuuuuuuuuuunnnnnnnnn !!!!!!!

all i want to do is

d
 r
  o
    p   i
        n
          t
            o
                a

                      h
              e.   o
                l

ALL I WANT TO DO IS YELL!

Expressing Feelings

If you keep stuffing your feelings inside you and not admitting they exist, they will come out all at once in a storm of inappropriate anger, or they may attack you inside and come out as depression or anxiety. It is important to let your feelings out in a way that hurts no one else.

Good ways of dealing with feelings include: talking to a trusted person, exercising, writing your feelings in a journal or a poem, or dealing with your feelings at the time they occur, so they don't get overwhelming.

Write down a list of ways you could do a better job of dealing with anger and frustration.

Write what you are feeling right now into the small box below. If you want to keep writing, grab a big piece of paper and write! Or find a creative place to write: on a piece of cardboard, on a piece of cloth, or with chalk on the sidewalk! *(Just not on your desk at school or on the bathroom wall!)*

My poem was called *All I Want.* Why don't you try to write a poem with that same title. What exactly do *you* want?

I REALLY LIKE THAT WORD "SMUG" FROM
THE "HOW DO I FEEL TODAY" POEM.

I HAD TO ASK MY MOM WHAT IT MEANT, AND
SHE LOOKED AT ME, AND SAID, "WELL, OF
ALL PEOPLE, YOU SHOULD KNOW."

TURNS OUT IT MEANS I KNOW I'M GOOD AT
WHAT I DO, BUT I LET EVERYBODY ELSE
KNOW IT TOO, AND WITH ATTITUDE.

SO I FIGURED I DON'T NEED TO DO THAT.
IF THEY ALREADY KNOW, THEN I'M
BETTER OFF NOT SHOWING THAT
"BETTER-THAN-YOU" SIDE OF ME.

LET 'EM DISCOVER IT THEMSELVES.
THEN THEY CAN TELL ME, NOT ME TELL
THEM, AND IT'D WORK OUT BETTER FOR
EVERYBODY, I THINK.

- FRANKIE

Now write about your story! Are you like Frankie? Would she be your friend, or not? Why or why not? Does her story bring up things that remind you of your own story?

Be free here to write whatever you like, or draw a picture if it is easier for you to express yourself that way.

MY STORY:

PART TWO

BUILDING SELF-UNDERSTANDING

AN ACROSTIC POEM!

A N ACROSTIC POEM

C AN BE GREAT FUN TO WRITE.

R HYME ISN'T IMPORTANT, BUT THE

O RDER OF THE LETTERS IS!

S EE, ON THE LEFT SIDE,

T HE LETTERS ALL SPELL "ACROSTIC"

I T'S EASY TO WRITE THESE POEMS -

C OME ON, NOW. YOU TRY IT!

Can you describe yourself?

Sometimes writing is the best way to put our thoughts and feelings together.

Lots of people, from entrepreneurs to poets use *acrostic poems* to express concepts, feelings and much more. Try taking any word and writing it down the length of the page (see the simple example on the previous page). Then write a phrase based on each starting letter.

A word that people commonly use when they are writing acrostics is their first name. (This is also a great gift to give someone you care about - write their name, and put nice things about them on every line.)

Each line of an acrostic starts with one letter of the word you have chosen. In the example acrostic on the next page, I took the nickname I was called as a child (Cindy) and used each letter to write words that I think describe who I am.

Acrostic

C hanging every moment, but

I nside knowing who I am,

N ever wanting to be bored,

D efiant, (Some call it stubborn,)

Y elling from the inside. *(I call it poetry.)*

This is a picture from back when I was called *Cindy*. Now that I am grown up, my name is *Cynthia!*

Who Am I?

Write an acrostic in the box below using your own name.

Focus on *positive* aspects of yourself. Keep rewriting the acrostic until it best describes you. Does your poem reflect the mood you are in, or your real personality?

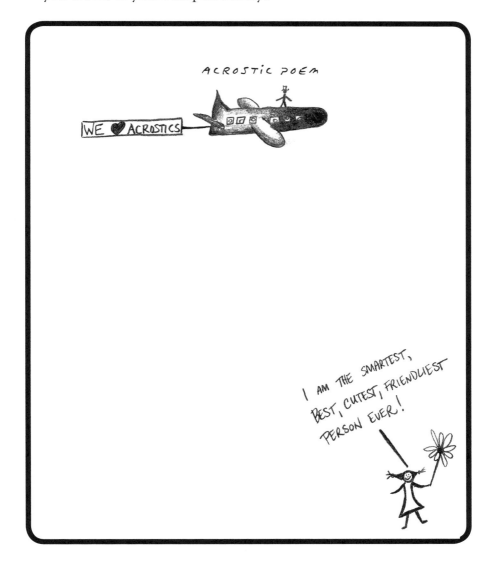

Now write another acrostic just like the last one, but instead of using your real name, use your nickname. For this one, choose a good nickname - something your parent or a good friend might call you!

ACROSTIC POEM WITH A GOOD NICKNAME

PEOPLE CALL ME "JULESY" BECAUSE "JULIA" DOESN'T SOUND LIKE ME AT ALL!

PEOPLE CALL ME "HOSS" BECAUSE I'M BIG, AND I PLAY FOOTBALL!

We all have nicknames that we don't like as much. Some of them are really hurtful, and some are just goofy or ridiculous. Write another acrostic poem here with that bad nickname, and try making that name into something good! The acrostic is a great way to do that! Have fun with this.

ACROSTIC POEM WITH A BAD NICKNAME

MY DAD CALLS ME NAMES THAT I CAN'T SAY HERE. THEY HURT ME EVERY TIME!

PEOPLE SOMETIMES CALL ME "SHRIMP" OR "SHORTY" BUT I DONT LIKE THAT!

Are you unique?

We all have parts of ourselves that make us unique. One person has a long nose, and someone else has a short one. Some people are tall, and others are short. That's what's so great about humans - we are all so different!

I am one of those people who is covered by moles! No, not the animals that burrow through the ground... I have a whole bunch of bumps that look like dark freckles all over my body. You might not think that's strange, but some people do!

During the late part of the 17th century in Massachussetts, during the Salem witch trials, moles (along with birthmarks and other such "blemishes") were considered signs that women were witches!

I still remember when I first read that fact! I was so glad I lived in modern times, and not back then. I wrote the poem on the next page when I was thinking about the tragic story of those women who were so much like me.

Even though we're not on trial as witches today, there are definitely things that people bully us about that we have no control over *(like moles!)*.

Moles

Did you know
they hanged people
who had moles?

Thought it
marked them
as a witch,

(not good to be a witch
in Salem, Massachusetts
three hundred years ago),

and if you said,
"I'm not a witch,
I didn't ask for moles,"

they still believed
you were marked
as evil.

No one listened.
No one cared.
You got killed anyway,

because people
with moles
are scary.

They're different.
They're witches, and no
matter what you wish

only time
will change
their minds.

Moles don't go away,
don't fade, like freckles.
They mark you.

THAT'S INTENSE!

Differences

Are you bullied because of something you have no control over? Or do you bully others because of something they cannot change?

Have you ever judged others by beauty, ugliness, skin tone, their abilities (coordination, intelligence), their age, gender, race or the family they come from? Have they ever done the same to you?

In order not to bully or be bullied, we need to accept first what is different (and not bad) about ourselves, and then what is different (and not bad) about others around us. In fact, differences can really be good!

Write a list of things that are different about you. Focus on things that are good, but it's alright if you list a few "bad" things as well.

I'M SO DIFFERENT (AND THAT'S A GOOD THING!)

AM I DIFFERENT?   DEFINITELY

Now get creative with those attributes you wrote down on the previous page. Write a poem or a journal entry called *My Differences Make Me Unique!*

MY DIFFERENCES MAKE ME UNIQUE!

I'M GREAT AT TENNIS!

Take the same list of attributes that you made, and now write another poem or journal entry using the word that describes you *better* than any of the other words.

THE WORD THAT DESCRIBES ME BEST IS...

You KNOW
I'M SWEET!

How do you react?

I've been a therapist for families, kids and teens for a long time, and believe me, people come to me nearly every day who have been hurt by others, in big and small ways, both physically and mentally.

There are just as many ways to react to being hurt as there are *ways* of getting hurt. Some people, after they've been hurt by someone they care about - maybe their parents, or their spouse - or by a bully at school, just feel like running away and hiding from the world. We've all felt like hiding from difficult situations, but this is much harder - they often just don't know who they can trust.

If you know anyone in that situation, or if you feel that way yourself, it's very important to know that there are people out there who care about you, and you must always keep your safety as your number one priority. After you feel safe, then you can begin to think about the world around you.

If

If I could fly and had feathers bright
I'd live in king's courtyards by day and by night;
I'd perch on a branch and sing at will
And all around would know my trill.
They'd say of me with the greatest pride,
She's the prettiest bird from far and wide.

Or if I could fly but had feathers brown
I might hide in a branch and watch the town,
And no one would guess and no one would see
That I was a spy from my spot in the tree.
I'd hear when they shouted. I'd know when they lied.
I' d see when they hit, and I'd cringe when they cried.

But sometimes I feel that if I knew how to fly
I'd just go away as far as the sky,
Where no one could say things that hurt my heart,
A place I could live and get a new start,
And no one would know, and no one could find
Where I lived on my own in the clouds of my mind.

What is Important to Me?

Envisioning a new world involves thinking about your own value system. How do you want to live from day to day?

Think about questions like: Is it okay to use others to advance yourself? Is it okay to see harm and do nothing about it? Is it okay to allow someone else to harm you or your family? Is it okay to just run away?

Choose a feeling that is stuck inside you and write it out so it shows how you feel. Use colored pens or markers to add to the intensity of the feeling. Use the boxes below to start, and then continue on a separate piece of paper if you feel inspired!

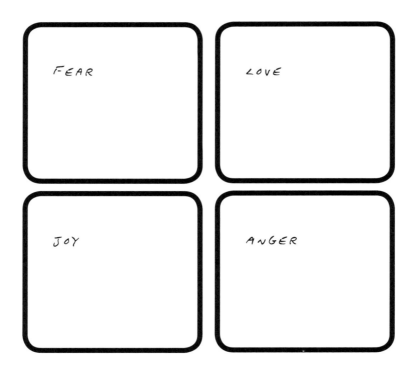

Write about the stuck-inside feelings you listed on the previous page! If you can't think of anything to write, draw here!

HERE'S WHAT I FEEL ABOUT:

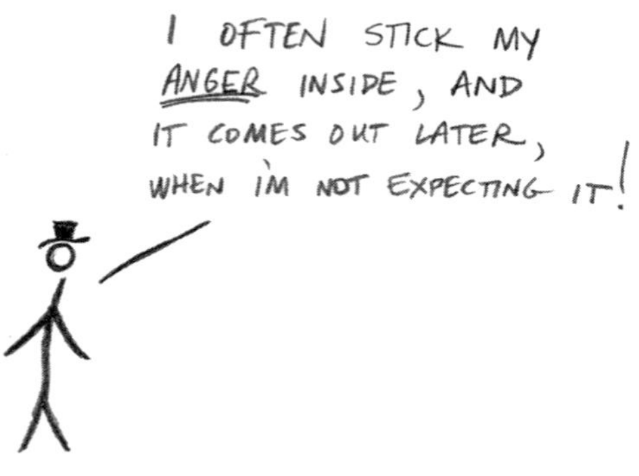

I OFTEN STICK MY
ANGER INSIDE, AND
IT COMES OUT LATER,
WHEN I'M NOT EXPECTING IT!

Look a few pages back at the poem *If*. Read the lines that start with "If I could fly..." Have you ever wished you could fly, or had dreams about flying? If not, have you ever flown in an airplane? Write a poem entitled *If I Could Fly*.

IF I COULD FLY

IF YOU CAN FLY,
WRITE "IF I COULD TALK!"
LOL!

THERE'S THIS FEELING STUCK INSIDE ME,
AND WHEN IT NAGS AT ME, I FEEL AWFUL.

IT'S THIS VOICE THAT SAYS, "YOU DO
EVERYTHING YOU'RE SUPPOSED TO DO, OR
TRY ANYWAY, AND YOU STILL MESS UP, AND
YOU STILL HAVE KIDS MAKING FUN OF YOU."

THE VOICE KEEPS TALKING: "IT DOESN'T
MATTER WHAT YOU DO, BECAUSE YOU'RE
STILL NOT COOL, YOU'RE STILL NOT LOOKED
UP TO, YOU'RE STILL PICKED ON, AND LOOKED
DOWN AT."

BUT NOW I KNOW HOW TO TALK BACK.

I SAY, "SHUT UP, VOICE. I DO WHAT I CAN,
AND MY FRIENDS THINK I'M COOL, AND I'M
OKAY WITH WHO I AM."

- G.W.

Now write about your story! Are you like G.W.? Would he be part of your group of friends? Why or why not? Does his story bring up things that remind you of your own story?

Be free here to write whatever you like, or draw a picture if it is easier for you to express yourself that way.

MY STORY:

PART THREE

ACTING ASSERTIVELY

A LIMERICK

I WRITE LIMERICK POEMS FOR FUN,

I NEVER CAN STOP AT JUST ONE.

YOU RHYME THE FIRST LINE

WITH LINES TWO AND FIVE

AND THEN YOUR LIMERICK IS DONE!

We all know complainers!

Do you know people who complain all the time, and never do anything to fix the things they complain about? I think we all do!

I wrote the poem on the next page in the form of a limerick, an old fashioned kind of poem that is often funny, but tells us something important. The poems have five lines, and the first, second and fifth line rhyme with each other. It's fun to write limericks, and they (almost) always turn out funny!

The limerick I wrote is about a girl I dreamed up named Nanette, who does nothing but complain (fret), even though she has all kinds of nice clothes to wear! The poem is meant to be simple and clever, but delivers a message at the same time: Nanette is too worried!

WHY WAS NANETTE NERVOUS?

Limerick

There was a young girl named Nanette
Who wore a pink party barrette
With her dress-up clothes
And shoes full of bows
And did nothing whatever, but fret.

NO ONE BULLIES
A LEPRECHAUN!
(OR DO THEY?)

Who Am I?

Nanette worries about everything, but never takes action. That is what we call being "passive". That means that you accept whatever is given to you, whether it is right or wrong.

If someone hurts a friend of yours, do you feel angry inside, but stay quiet? If a bully steals your lunch money, do you say nothing and starve at lunchtime?

Think about a time when you were "passive" about something, and you are still angry about the outcome. What could have been done differently? Write about it below.

I WAS PASSIVE WHEN...

Describe or draw a situation where someone *really* made you mad!! What did you do (or *not* do) about it?

What could or should you have said in that situation you described on the previous page (where you got really mad), that might have been a better way to react?

I COULD HAVE SAID...

I WISH I WOULD HAVE SAID:
"STOP BEING A BULLY!"

The "little" lie

When I was eleven years old, my best friend told a lie about me one morning. By lunchtime no one would sit by me. I didn't even know why everyone was mad at me.

By the second day there were two groups of people: the ones who believed me, and the ones who believed her.

The incredible thing about this incident is that those two groups stayed that way until I graduated from high school and left home. That "little" lie affected me every day of my school life that year.

Those kinds of incidents happen much more often in today's world via social media, and the consequences can be lifelong, and unfortunately, sometimes even deadly.

If you know anyone, even if they aren't your friend, who is being bullied online or in person, you might be *saving their life* if you tell an adult about it. So don't hesitate to "tell on someone" if it might help someone else survive.

The Lie

It's a lie! lie! *lie!*
Oh why, why, *why?*
Can't even try, try, *try*
to say what really happened.

What's really sad, sad, *sad,*
is she's not so bad, bad, *bad,*
but only mad, mad, *mad*
that I got a better grade.

It's such a lie, lie, *lie,*
and I cry, cry, *cry*
as I try to *deny*
those ugly words she said.

I'm not a cheat, a dirty *cheat,*
got no heat, heat, *heat,*
or have to try and *beat*
anybody else.

It's a lie, lie, *lie!*
They won't listen as I *try*
to explain why, why, *why,*
and say what really happened.

Aggressive Behavior

Aggressive behavior does not just mean starting a fistfight with someone. It doesn't even have to involve touching anyone else. Telling lies and spreading gossip is also aggressive behavior. It can cause emotional scars and even suicide.

Besides the negative consequences for the bullied person, aggressive behavior also gets the bully in trouble, since aggression often involves breaking laws and rules. And sometimes, it can even involve a lifetime of guilt. Imagine how terrible you could feel if you had done something that might make someone want to hurt themselves.

Write about a time when you might have acted like a bully, perhaps to a sibling or a neighbor. What were the consequences of your aggression? Did you achieve what you wanted? Would there have been a better way to achieve a positive outcome?

I THINK I MIGHT HAVE ACTED LIKE A BULLY...

Has anyone ever written about you in a negative way online? Have you ever written something negative about someone else on a social network or some other public place? Cyber-bullying is something that we didn't have to contend with when I was a child, and it's something that can really damage people's lives. Write about a time that you wrote something online about someone else in a public space.

ONE TIME, I WROTE...

Have you ever sent an angry or upset email or text message that you wish you could have taken back after you clicked "Send"? Did that email or text message hurt a friend? What did that feel like? Did you stop being friends after that? How, if at all, did you solve that situation, or if not, how *could* you have solved it without sending that angry message?

I COULD HAVE WRITTEN...

LEMONADE

INGREDIENTS:

      THE LEMONS LIFE GIVES US

      1 BIG CUP OF SUGAR

      1 BIG PORTION OF
      ASSERTIVE BEHAVIOR

STIR ALL INGREDIENTS, THEN ENJOY!

Lemonade!

D o you know people who can have anything happen to them, and they always recover quickly? They're the ones who are given lemons by life, and they make lemonade.

How do they do it? Could it be because of "attitude"? Or is there something deeper? Are they just lucky?

I wrote the poem on the next page about a resilient kid who is good at "making the best of things."

Resilience

When I fall
I get back up.
I don't like mud.

Like a cat
with nine lives
I refuse to give in.

If you call me
a "fathead" –
I'll call you a "thud!"

I'm a very
special person –
and I intend to win!

If I'm sick
in my bed
I'll enjoy chicken soup,

Watch TV
and relax.
That's how I recoup.

Push my head
beneath the water
and bubbles I will blow.

Call me names –
I'll just laugh.
They won't hurt me. NO!

Assertive Behavior

If it doesn't help to be passive, and we get in trouble when we are aggressive, then what is the best way to act? The answer is, act *assertively*.

Acting assertively means we need to act honestly, express our feelings in a way that will not hurt others, and include factual information. The person in the poem *Resilience* has a positive attitude. She asks herself, "How can I make the most of this situation?" Write about how *you* can be more assertive.

I COULD HAVE WRITTEN...

What can you say to a person who pushes ahead of you in line? Try not to call him/her names, don't remain silent, don't shout, don't use your elbow or kick to get their attention.

Instead, try to state the facts solidly, and expect them to respond. What would that sound like? Write that conversation below! Start your conversation with: "Excuse me..."

"EXCUSE ME..."

Now write a conversation between two other people in the same situation. Pretend that you are watching, and a bully cuts in front of someone in line. What can the person say to the bully? Can they come to some agreement?

THIS BULLY BUDGES IN LINE...

THERE WAS A YOUNG GIRL WHO WAS SMART,
WHO NEVER THOUGHT SHE WAS A PART
OF THE PEER GROUP HER AGE,
AND IT FILLED HER WITH RAGE,
UNTIL SHE TALKED TO THEM
STRAIGHT FROM HER HEART.

- EMMY

Now write about your story! Are you like Emmy? Have you ever been assertive, and been able to tell people what you think? Why or why not? Does his story bring up things that remind you of your own story?

Be free here to write whatever you like, or draw a picture if it is easier for you to express yourself that way.

MY STORY:

PART FOUR

RESPONDING TO AUTHORITY

I've had enough!

D o you feel as though there is always someone barking out orders at you? I remember thinking when I was a kid that those orders would stop when I became an adult. But the orders just come from different people now!

There is a good way and a bad way to ask people to do things, and to accept orders from people who are important in your life. It is vital that we learn these skills in order to succeed in school, within our workplaces, with our friends, and within our families.

The poem I wrote on the next page comes from all of the children I've had in my practice who have simply *had enough!*

Taking Orders

"Do this!" Dad reminds,
"Do that!" "Rake the leaves."
"Finish the dishes!" Sister whines,
"Feed the cat!" I'm her pet peeve.
"Pick up clothes!" Brother's worse.
"Find that book!" He always shouts.
"Get your coat That's it! I've *had* it!
off that hook!" I'm moving *out!*

Orders that
come as shouting
just encourage
endless pouting.
I'd really like
to go out and play
and not do any more
today.

Mom asserts,
"Do what you're told,"
but I am ready
to major explode.
Teacher demands,
"Sit still."
Grandma says,
"Swallow your pill."

How to Give and Take Orders

Is there a *better* way to give orders than the way the characters in the poem *Taking Orders* do it? Sometimes, asking a person nicely, to repeat what they are asking you to do, would be appropriate. Sometimes it doesn't change anything, but you would at least be modeling assertiveness. Write some orders that you hear every day in a list below.

ORDERS PEOPLE SHOUT AT ME:

Translate the orders from your list on the previous page to how you would *like* to be spoken to! Write a conversation or poem below.

"WOULD YOU PLEASE..."

"WOULD YOU,
COULD YOU,
VERY POSSIBLY,
PERHAPS...
IF YOU HAVE ENERGY,
THINK ABOUT CLEANING
JUST A SMALL
CORNER OF YOUR ROOM?"

What it comes down to is this: bullies demand, and healthy people ask politely. If you are the one who is asking, you will probably get a better result if you do it assertively, not aggressively.

Name something in your life that you ask others to do for you. How do you ask? How do they respond? Write a dialogue between you and one of those people.

"IT WOULD BE FANTASTIC IF..."

Hard to love

A very common way to experience bullying is from within your own family. We don't talk about it much, because we have to *live with* those people! Just know that if you or someone else you know has *any* problems with a family member, go to someone you *trust*, whether that be a favorite teacher or your school counselor.

Our parents tell us that we are supposed to love our brothers and sisters, but sometimes they are the hardest to love, because of the way they treat us.

In the poem on the next page, the child is very happy to get rid of her five big sisters. Or is she?

Five Big Sisters

Five big sisters
sitting on the floor,
one fell through
and then there were four.

Four big sisters
watching over me,
a whale ate one
and then there were three.

Three big sisters
with clothes so new,
one moved out
and then there were two.

Two big sisters
having fun,
one ate a mushroom
and then there was one.

One big sister
on her daily run,
never came back
and then there were none.

No big sisters
telling me what's right,
I can run and jump
and stay up all night.

No big sisters
telling me what to do,
I'm on my own.
Is this the right shoe?!

Siblings as Bullies

Name a sister, brother, cousin or other family member or close friend of the family who always tells you what to do. Does he or she act like a bully, or was he or she just trying to help you? (*Or were you the older sibling who told others what to do?*)

When do we have to obey authority figures, whether they are family members or teachers, bosses, or police? And who is to say that they *are* authority figures?

Who do you look up to as *real* authority figures? List them below.

REAL AUTHORITY FIGURES:

One way to respond to authority figures is to first say to yourself, "Do what they say, but do it *your* way."

Now list a few people who take authority over you even though you think they shouldn't! What do you say to those people?

Write a letter to your sister, brother, cousin, step-dad or whom-ever you would like, and express how their bullying has affected you, or that you now understand how your bullying affected them.

Remember, this is for your own understanding *only*. In most cases it is better *not* to ever send this letter.

DEAR...

MY MOM DOESN'T SAY, "DO WHAT YOU'RE TOLD..."

SHE SAYS... "HEY..." WELL, I CAN'T WRITE DOWN WHAT SHE SAYS!

IT MAKES ME SO MAD AND IT EXPLODES INSIDE OF ME LIKE A BALLOON PUMPED UP WITH AIR, OR A BASKETBALL OR SOMETHING. I JUST WANT TO YELL AT ANYBODY ELSE, BECAUSE I CAN'T EVER SAY ANYTHING TO MY MOM WITHOUT HER GETTING SO MAD SHE TURNS PURPLE IN THE FACE!

FUNNY, YOU KNOW, I FEEL BETTER ALREADY. IT'S HARD TO WRITE IT, BUT, ONCE I DO, IT ALMOST FEELS LIKE I'M TALKING TO SOMEONE REAL.

- CHARLES

Now write about your story! Does Charles look like someone you would go talk to across the room on the first day of classes? Does his story bring up things that remind you of your own story?

Be free here to write whatever you like, or draw a picture if it is easier for you to express yourself that way.

MY STORY:

PART FIVE

ACTING WITH COMPASSION

Do you love pizza?

It's very strange that the same word "love" is used for simple things like "loving" pizza, and important and big things like loving people. We just know that the two meanings are different, even though we use the same word.

Even when we theoretically know what the word "love" means, and we say it to someone, it means different things to different people. That's why there are so many movies and TV shows that dwell on themes like: "does she really love me?"

We all ask ourselves from time to time, "Does anyone really love me?" How can we know for sure? We also think, "Can someone stop loving me?"

The most important thing to keep in mind is that we should act out of love for others, and not just for ourselves. If we can do that, things will change for the better in our lives.

You Know What I Wish?

Thanks for the oatmeal cooking since six,
for the nuts and the berries you cut up and fixed,
the orange juice you squeezed and the toast I see.
But what I want to know is: Do you love me?

My clothes are washed and folded and hung.
My sores are soothed when I'm cut up or stung.
You get me to bed. You wake me up too.
But I want to know: Do you love me? Do you?

You tell me you love me, but what does that mean?
Will you love me if I fail to keep my room clean?
Will you love me if I'm ugly, or if we never agree?
How do I know if you really love me?

The dog wags his tail as I bring treats up the path.
My friends all love me 'cause I finish their math.
The cat only purrs when I put out her fish.
Do you know what I want? Do you know what I wish?

I want you to think of me when you see the sun rise,
to see me in your dreams behind the lids of your eyes,
to smile when I'm happy, to soar when I'm free.
And if you cry when I'm sad, then I'll know you love me.

Are You Loved? How Can You Love Others?

Have you heard the phrase, "Hurt people hurt people"? Think about it for one moment. Bullies are often people who have been hurt by others. In other words, bullies can be victims too.

You Know What I Wish? asks the universal question: "Do you really love me?" Everyone asks this question, and everyone wants to be loved by *someone*.

We can choose to love others, or at least be polite to others, even if we have not felt perfect love. What do you love?

I GUESS I "LOVE" THESE PEOPLE IN MY LIFE:

Now try writing down a list of the *things* you love, and then the *animals* and *anything else* you love.

THINGS I LOVE:

ANIMALS I LOVE:

ANYTHING ELSE I LOVE:

I LOVE,
YOU LOVE,
WE ALL LOVE
ICE CREAM!

How are they and the things you love on the previous page the same? How are they different? How have you treated them in the past? How will you improve on your "loving" behavior?

While thinking about this, write a poem or journal entry, and see what you come up with.

I LOVE...

Most important words

The most important words in any friendship or relationship are probably not *I love you*. They are *I'm sorry*.

It's incredibly important to apologize and ask for forgiveness if you know that you have hurt another person.

I have written a poem in the voice of a young person who has done something wrong, and is apologizing to another person. Again, I used the acrostic style of poem, listing the letters of the words "I'm sorry."

I'm Sorry

I forget sometimes

My problems can cause a fight.

So forgive me, please,

Or I won't be able to sleep tonight.

Really, I care.

Rarely do I apologize, but

You are important, and you were right.

Forgiving Others and Self

If you forgive or befriend the person who bullies you, how might that change his/her behavior?

What would befriending a bully look like? Does it mean you would become an accomplice to his/her aggressive acts?

BEFRIENDING A BULLY

APOLOGIES ROCK!

What would forgiving yourself look like? How will your own actions change if you forgive yourself?

IF I WERE TO FORGIVE MYSELF...

I FORGIVE ME!

Write an acrostic using the word "forgive". Work on the lines of the poem until they express your feelings just right.

FORGIVE

4-GIVE?
WHAT ABOUT
1, 2 and 3-GIVE!?
LOL!

Who owns the beach?

Do you ever wish that the world belonged to you and it would follow your command? That's kind of how I was feeling when I wrote the poem on the next page about pinfish.

I was fishing in the Gulf of Mexico and none of the fish cooperated with me. And when I walked the beach, even the crabs wouldn't do what I wanted. I call them thieves in the poem, because they had a different idea about who owned the beach than I did. I didn't have the control that I wanted!

Think about "command" and "control" while you read the poem and work on the exercises in this section.

Thieves

Blasted pinfish steals
shrimp bait meant for
flounder, then pricks
his pins into my flesh
as I set him free.
It's Sunday and I
don't need his trouble.

When I walk the beach
I receive no gift
from the sea —
the empty shell houses
a hermit crab
who stole it first,
and challenges me to a duel.

Thieves they are —
refusing to respect
my ownership of shrimp
and empty shell,
of ocean swell
and all the sands
that fall and fall
and shift and scratch

and finally catch
in my tight
leather shoe.

Command & Control

Do you feel as though you should be in control of everything in your life? Are you angry when you might not have complete command of the situation?

In *Thieves*, how are you like or unlike the hermit crab who has no home of its own unless it steals an empty shell? To find out more about them, search on the Internet or your local library. They are amazing animals who carry their homes around on their backs.

Write a poem that describes what you feel about being in control or out of control, and how you are learning to switch from one to the other.

I AM LIKE A...

When have you been in control? Describe a few situations below.

I WAS iN CONTROL WHEN...

When have you not been in control? Describe a few situations below.

I WAS NOT IN CONTROL WHEN...

ANYTIME
MY DAD IS
AROUND!

Because I'm shy I don't talk when
Everybody else visits.
Friendship is hard — it's easier to
Run or play volleyball. But now...
I choose to change. I will
Engage others, even if it's hard, and
Not stay alone. Friendship is now my
Daily workout.

- CHAR

Now write about your story! Are you like Char? Do you need to be more compassionate to other people sometimes? Why or why not? Does her story bring up things that remind you of your own story?

Be free here to write whatever you like, or draw a picture if it is easier for you to express yourself that way.

MY STORY:

PART SIX

DEVELOPING INNER STRENGTH

Any name can be made fun of!

It doesn't matter what your parents did to try to name you with a "tough" or "pretty" name – there will always be ways of making fun of your name, if someone tries hard enough!

In the next poem, I mention that I was called "Scholar" in school. At first I thought it was a compliment, but when everyone started to laugh, I realized they were making fun of me, because girls in those days weren't supposed to be smart. They were supposed to be good homemakers, and didn't have to be smart. But I was different, so they called me "Scholar". I was proud at first, until I realized that the others hadn't meant the nickname as a good thing!

I didn't like that the other kids made fun of me, but I didn't change my behavior either. I was secretly happy that they thought I was smart, and I knew that it was *just* as important for girls to be "scholars" as it was for boys!

"Girl"

Poor Carol Jim
I feel bad for him.

The boys call him "Girl",
the girls stay away —

He fights all the time
just to get through the day.

His head is almost always
bowed to the the ground —

His shoulders are slumped
and he wears a stony frown.

I told him he should use
his second name, Jim,

but the kids still remember,
and keep teasing him.

I know how he feels
'cause they call me "Scholar"

You want to *run,*
You want to *holler*!

Poor Carol Jim
I feel bad for him.

Name Calling

Has it happened to you? Or have you been the one who calls others bad names?

The nursery rhyme about "sticks and stones" is true. They can't hurt you if you won't allow it. If you are a boy and your name is Carol, then look up on the computer and find other men with that name. If they call you "Scholar", then let them know that it is a compliment to you, and thank you very much. It's all in your attitude. Take it with humor. It's okay to go home and cry, but don't do it front of a bully.

Can you visualize yourself as strong? Close your eyes and experience the bully calling you a name. How will you respond?

THE BULLY CALLED ME...

CALL ME "GIRL" AND I'LL FIGHT!

Write down all of the nicknames others have called you through-out your life. There are tons of them! Think about what your parents called you as a child, what your friends call you, and what you call yourself! Is there a family nickname that you and a parent share? List them all here, and write whether they are positive or negative nicknames.

MY NICKNAMES:

Now, try to make up a bunch of new nicknames for yourself, and for the people around you who have "bad" nicknames. List them here and explain why you are changing those nicknames to something new!

NEW NICKNAMES:

Do people always underestimate you?

D o bullies or even friends ever look at you and laugh, thinking that you aren't as good as they are? At sports, or in a competition, or in appearance?

My husband has always been a great athlete, since the time we met in college. The funny thing is, when he showed up at running races, he never wore what all of the other runners wore; he didn't have the fancy clothes and neon shoes. He always showed up with a simple t-shirt and regular old shorts. Everyone looked right past him, not thinking that he would be a challenge. And then he would zoom by them in the race, and they would be astonished.

You can listen to bullies, but then you should realize that you can be like an ant! (Yes, that's what I wrote - an ant. Read the poem I wrote on the next page, about Tiny, the ant, and you will know what I mean.)

Tiny, the Little Ant

Tiny, the little ant
scurry, scurry, scurries.
No one notices
he's in such a hurry.

Ants, like Tiny,
don't know they're small,
and do what they do
without worrying at all.

He climbs ten foot walls,
carries crumbs on his back,
finds sugar on the table,
and never loses his track.

Tiny understands
he can do anything,
and if someone tries to stop him –
well—he just might sting!

So What If I'm Different?

Tiny doesn't care if he is bigger or smaller than any other ant. He just hurries about his business, and accomplishes a *ton* every day!

Think about what makes you different or unique. Why is it good or bad? Do you say, "I'm different, but that's good"?

I AM DIFFERENT, BUT THAT'S GOOD!

Tiny doesn't want to hurt anyone, but if someone tries to stop him, he might just sting. What kind of stinger do you have? What kind of sting is okay, and what kind of sting is off-limits? Write a poem or journal entry entitled *Stinger*.

Are you like an ant, or a different kind of animal? Write about your animal in a poem or journal entry.

I AM LIKE A...

I Used to Be

I used to be a wild crocus, rough-edged,
tough to be the first up in spring,
fed by melting snow,
growing timidly in
pale violet hues
between
rock clusters
on exposed hillsides.
It was hard to find me.
You had to explore.
But I bloomed anyway,
whether you found me or not.

But now
I am domestic,
growing in my own
garden, and my crocus color
is bright. I am still the first to bloom
after the snow, but hybridizing has smoothed
my edges.
My color now
shouts: Here I am.

Change

Choose something in nature to describe yourself as you used to be. Then continue on, describing how you are now.

I WAS LIKE A...

NOW I AM...

I WAS A KLUTZY GIRAFFE, AND NOW I AM A RUNNING DEER!

Let's do another one of these exercises. But this time, use *simile*. That means, you should use the word "like". For example, *"I was like a big bear, and now I am like a little mouse!"*

I WAS LiKE A...

NOW I AM LiKE A...

Let's use this exercise one last time. This time we will use *metaphor*. That means, you pretend you *are* the thing you compare yourself to. For example, *"I am now a lion, though I used to be a cat."*

I AM NOW A...

I USED TO BE A...

I USED TO BE A LITTLE CHOCOLATE CANDY
THAT MELTED IN EVERYBODY'S HAND. ALL
I NEEDED WAS A FISTFUL OF PRESSURE
AND I FELL APART.

BUT NOW I HAVE READ IN SOME SCIENTIFIC
ARTICLES THAT CHOCOLATE IS GOOD FOR
US. AND MY MOTHER SAYS THAT THE BEST
CHOCOLATE IS MADE WITH BUTTER THAT
MELTS EASILY.

I HOPE I'M BECOMING ONE OF THOSE
CHOCOLATES THAT PEOPLE PAY A LOT OF
MONEY FOR. OR MAYBE I'M STILL A SMALL
PIECE OF CANDY, BUT ONE THAT HAS AN
ALMOND IN THE CENTER. ALMONDS ARE
SUPPOSED TO HELP YOU LIVE LONGER!

- MARTY

Now write about your story! Do you melt easily like Marty used to? Would he be part of your group of friends? Why or why not? Does his story bring up things that remind you of your own story?

Be free here to write whatever you like, or draw a picture if it is easier for you to express yourself that way.

MY STORY:

PART SEVEN

LEARNING TO COMMUNICATE

Conversation bullies

I am sure that you know someone who is very difficult to talk with! It may be a parent or grandparent, or it may be a teacher or principal. It could even be your best friend!

Some people are conversation bullies and really don't allow anyone else to get a word in edgewise. Not only do they keep others from talking, they also do not listen, and that can be frustrating, and even hurtful to others.

The poem on the next page is a conversation poem, and the ALL-CAPS letters represent SHOUTING by one of the participants in the conversation.

Waiting to Be Heard

"Can I say something now?"

"OF COURSE. I'M LISTENING.
DON'T KNOW WHY YOU HAVE
SO MUCH TROUBLE TALKING TO ME.
SAY WHAT YOU WILL."

"I was thinking about how. . . "

"DON'T SAY I ALWAYS
HURT YOUR FEELINGS –
AND DON'T SAY
I DON'T CARE . . . "

"I just wanted to share . . ."

"AND IF YOU START IN ABOUT
ME PREACHING – YOU'RE RIGHT,
I WON'T LISTEN – SO GO AHEAD NOW.
SAY WHAT YOU WANTED TO SAY."

(She started to cry.)

"COME ON NOW. IT'S YOUR TURN –
HOW DO YOU EXPECT US TO
COMMUNICATE WHEN YOU
DON'T EVEN TRY?"

Who Am I?

Some people act like bullies when they talk. They don't listen and only allow others to respond in a very controlled way. Think about some conversations you have had. Are you ever like that?

SOMETIMES I'M A CONVERSATION BULLY...

If there is someone who is a conversation bully to you, write a letter to him/her about how this hurts you. *(Keep this letter private. It is for you, not for them.)*

DEAR...

Now write a letter to someone whom you might have (accidentally or on purpose) bullied in a conversation. *(Again, keep this
letter private. It's for you, not them.)*

DEAR...

Grieving goose

Do you remember haiku poems from school? The form comes from Japan and is in three lines, although now people sometimes write them with fewer rules, such as without the exact number of syllables.

I decided to write the little haiku on the following page when I saw a Canada goose honking in the middle of the road, with cars screeching around it, and with no one stopping or seemingly even caring that this goose's life-mate had been killed by a speeding car.

The grieving goose was honking very loudly, and still no one heard it. I felt very sad for the goose, but of course, there was nothing I could do. I felt helpless.

Haiku

The Canada goose
pacing near its road-kill mate
honks at speeding cars

Making Yourself Heard

The poor goose in my haiku honked, and no one seemed to listen to the story he was trying to tell about his grief. All people heard was "honk honk honk..."

How do you get people to listen to you? Do you make your voice louder? Or softer (so they have to listen to hear you)? Do you change the time or location of when you choose to say things? Do you change whom you are communicating with?

What ways of communicating do we have, other than "honking" at one another? List a few ways that we can get our message across to one another more effectively.

SOME GREAT WAYS TO COMMUNICATE:

YOU ROCK!
KEEP IT UP!

Write a haiku beginning: "I open my mouth . . ." Write several versions of it - get creative! The form is very simple: 5-7-5. That means, put 5 syllables in the first line, 7 syllables in the second, and 5 syllables in the third! No rhyme or anything else necessary. Have fun with this!

I OPEN MY MOUTH...

BIG HAPPY FAMILY?

Connecting with family and friends

I really enjoy using social media networks to connect with family and friends. I check in every morning to see what everyone has uploaded or written during the last several hours.

As great a tool as social media networks can be in our lives, they can also be very damaging. We all know stories of people who have been seriously hurt by so-called "friends" on the Internet. Cyberbullying is a growing problem each year, as the Internet plays a bigger and bigger role in our lives.

I wrote a little poem on the next page in my best attempt at "texting language". The bullying in the poem is very mild compared with the cyberbullying that actually happens on the web today. But you will get the general idea of what I mean!

On Facebook

Jenn
fyi – did u hear the news?
imho it's true:
she is a JERK
just like Sue

Jenn
so did i
but w an old dude 2
i don't want 2 hang w her
how bout u?

Anna
she = such a loser
i saw her @ th mall
hangin w the geeks
@ th north wall

Anna
u r 2 right
this is th end,
we shd txt her
#epicfail – unfriend!

Jenn
lol i know
i saw her 2,
+ i can guess
what they're gn t do!

Anna
yup – @ the end
of that long hall,
i thk i saw her
w that loser paul

Social Media Bullies

Have you been hurt by videos, social media messages, or text messages? Make a list of ways that you can prevent yourself and others from getting hurt in this way.

HOW TO PREVENT SOCIAL MEDIA BULLYING:

If you have been hurt by social media bullies, how can you repair your "image" online and in person? Don't forget that schools, police and parents can also help if someone has put out lies about you. It is also good to have a strong social network or people directly around you to support you in bad times and give you strength all the time.

If you have (either accidentally or on purpose) cyberbullied someone, examine your reasons for it. Why do you think you did it, and what could you do to prevent it the next time?

MY THOUGHTS ON CYBERBULLYING:

Write a conversation between two people in texting language, or with social media lingo. Use that conversation to talk about *stopping* lies about other people, as well as gossip and negative information that are all a part of cyberbullying!

FYi...

THE RED TAILED HAWK
WATCHING FROM THE CYPRESS TREE
WAITS TO POUNCE

ON THE LITTLE VOLE
RUNNING ACROSS THE MEADOW
UNAWARE, UNAFRAID.

— JULIA

Now write about your story! Do you connect to Julia's poem? Would she be part of your group of friends? Why or why not? Does her story bring up things that remind you of your own story?

Be free here to write whatever you like, or draw a picture if it is easier for you to express yourself that way.

MY STORY:

PART EIGHT

OUT INTO THE WORLD

The biggest bully

Sometimes the biggest bully of all is the weather, something that none of us can change.

Have you ever had to fight the wind to walk, or wear your winter coat and hat and gloves just to be able to go outside at all?

In the poem on the next page, I compare the wind to a bully. While you are reading the poem, think about other "bullies" in nature!

The Blustery Bullying Wind

This winter's been cold, so I've been mostly indoors,
but now it's March and I search through my drawers

for a lighter jacket and pair of old pants
that I can wear outside, and maybe by chance,

I'll find a crocus among the rocks out back,
or forsythia buds behind the falling-down shack.

I know it's too early for a new baby fawn,
but I just saw a robin pull a worm from my lawn.

The sun's shining bright, a wonderful surprise,
but the cold north wind blows dust in my eyes,

and my mouth and my nose, and I get all sneezy.
I want to be outside, but it's just not so easy.

Dry leaves fly past me, then the wind gives a shove
and blows the baseball right out of my glove.

(Reminds me of my neighbor, a bully named Hawk,
who always makes fun of the way I walk,

so I end up hiking blocks out of my way,
on the way to school every single day.)

But the wind is different. It comes and it goes,
and sometimes it's warm and gentle as it blows.

And by the end of March, it feels less like a bully,
and more like a lamb, warm and wooly.

So I dress for the wind, and know it won't last.
It's bringing springtime and flowers with each roaring blast.

What Do You Do With a Bully?

How can you prepare for interactions with a bully just as you would prepare for a windy or rainy day with different choices of clothes? Think about what you can do to avoid bullies in both the world of nature, and in your interactions with other humans.

Think about how you are bullied and/or how you at times bully others. Are there ways that you can change your attitude to make the bullying not influence your life every day? How can you rethink bullying? Write some thoughts below.

RETHINKING BULLYING:

Write a poem about another bully in nature besides the wind. Where do you fit in? Are you that natural bully, or does that bully affect you somehow? How does your poem end?

A BULLY IN NATURE

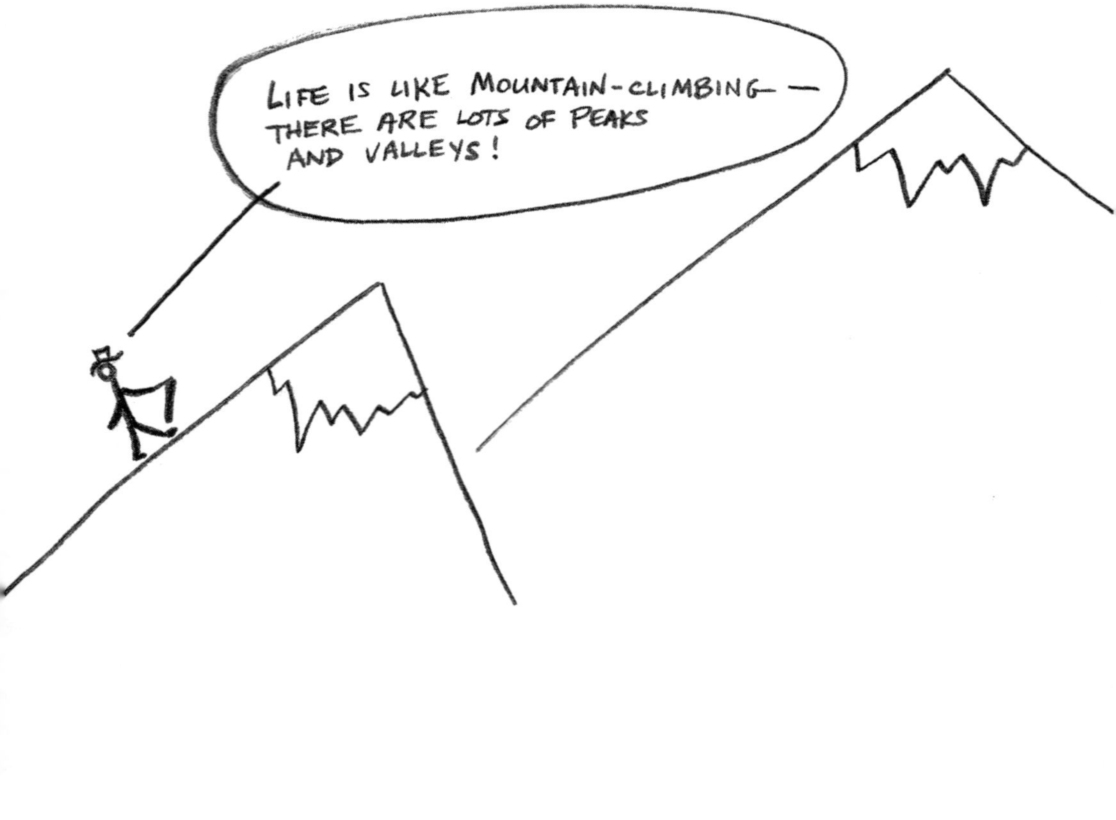
LIFE IS LIKE MOUNTAIN-CLIMBING — THERE ARE LOTS OF PEAKS AND VALLEYS!

What will you be like 20 years from now?

Do you ever wonder what you will be like 20 years from now? What about next month, or next week, or next year? What will you be like when you are old and gray? Will you be married with kids? Or will you be the oldest person to climb Mount Everest?

For the last poem and exercise in the book, I have saved my favorite. We did one like this in an earlier chapter, but it wasn't quite this focused on the future. I would really like you to think about what you are now, and what you would like to be in the future.

The brief poem on the next page is simple, yet it really talks about deep feelings and emotions, and shows what can happen if things go well.

I Am Now... But I Will Be...

I am now a raging stream full of
rocks and sand and sticks
carving out a new valley bed.

But I will be a crystal clear brook once again
when the rain drains into the grass
and sunlight comes out to dry my swollen tears.

I Am Now... But I Will Be...

Write three versions of this poem on the following pages. You will come up with new ideas each time. Remember, compare yourself to something that describes how you are now, and how you will be in the future.

I AM NOW...

BUT I WILL BE...

I'M LIKE
A BULLFROG

I AM NOW...

BUT I WILL BE...

I AM NOW...

BUT I WILL BE...

I THINK
I'M LIKE
A DAISY!

(THIS IS A LETTER TO FUTURE-ME)

DEAR ME!

THIS IS WHAT I KNOW. I NEVER TRY TO
HURT ANYBODY. I TRY TO MIND MY OWN
BUSINESS, BUT SOMETIMES PEOPLE GET IN
THE WAY. I HAVE TO TRY TO BE BETTER AT
NOT BULLYING PEOPLE.

YOU KNOW, IN FOOTBALL, I HAVE TO BLOCK
PEOPLE SO THE QUARTERBACK CAN GET
THROUGH. BUT YOU HAVE TO TRY TO STAY
WITHIN THE RULES, AND I SHOULD DO THAT
WITH PEOPLE, TOO.

WHEN THE RULES AREN'T REAL CLEAR,
THAT'S WHEN YOU ASK SOMEBODY SMARTER
THAN YOU, OR SOMEBODY YOU TRUST, LIKE
YOUR COACH.

- HOSS

Now write about your story! Are you like Hoss in any way? Could you sometimes be more sensitive to others? Does his story bring up things that remind you of your own story?

Be free here to write whatever you like, or draw a picture if it is easier for you to express yourself that way.

MY STORY:

NOTES

(AND DOODLES)

RESOURCES

(JUST A FEW TO START)

Government website targeting bullying
* *www.stopbullying.gov*

Non-profit website with moderated support groups
* *www.bullying.org*

STRYVE *(Striving to Reduce Youth Violence)*
* *www.cdc.gov/violenceprevention/stryve/*

"Bullying: It's Not Okay" – *healthychildren.org*
* *http://goo.gl/So49C*

American Academy of Pediatrics re: youth violence
* *http://goo.gl/2AszE*

"Stop Bullying in its Tracks" – p.19 *Healthy Children*
* *http://goo.gl/11RKV*

"Bullying Among...Students" – MMWR,
* *http://goo.gl/plgZk*

ABOUT THE
CONTRIBUTORS

CYNTHIA BLOMQUIST GUSTAVSON ACSW, LCSW, AUTHOR

DR. EDWARD E. GUSTAVSON MD, FAAP, FOREWORD

DR. KENT GUSTAVSON PHD, EDITOR & ILLUSTRATOR

Cynthia Blomquist Gustavson ACSW LCSW is the award-winning author of a dozen poetry, therapy, writing and children's books. She has been a practicing psychotherapist for 30 years, and has worked in drug prevention, practiced individual and group therapy, and worked extensively with caregivers of the chronically ill and developmentally disabled.

Dr. Edward E. Gustavson MD FAAP, a graduate of Harvard Medical School, is a practicing physician in Tulsa, Oklahoma, where he specializes in developmental pediatrics. He was recently awarded the 2011 Patients' Choice Award.

Dr. Kent Gustavson PhD, a graduate of the State University of New York at Stony Brook, and the former Faculty Director of the Leadership Development and Service Learning departments there, is the award-winning author of "Blind But Now I See", the biography of musician Doc Watson, and several other titles.

DON'T FORGET!
PEOPLE WILL BE
THERE TO HELP!

BE GOOD TO OTHERS
AND BE GOOD
TO YOURSELF!